THINGS
I LIKE

FIRST RHYMES
AND STORIES

Each story and poem in this collection has been
previously published by Walker Books

First published 2001 by Walker Books Ltd
87 Vauxhall Walk, London SE11 5HJ

2 4 6 8 10 9 7 5 3 1

© year of publication Shirley Hughes

This book has been typeset in Garamond

Printed in Hong Kong

British Library Cataloguing in Publication Data:
a catalogue record for this book
is available from the British Library

ISBN 0-7445-8176-1

Shirley Hughes
THINGS I LIKE
FIRST RHYMES AND STORIES

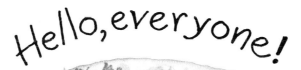

Hello, everyone!

WALKER BOOKS
AND SUBSIDIARIES
LONDON • BOSTON • SYDNEY

Contents

Introduction

The children in this collection, Katie and Olly, are not real. They come out of my imagination. But they seemed very real from  the first moment I drew them on the page. Olly has only just stopped being a baby, of course, and hasn't learned to speak properly yet. He speaks Olly language most of the time. But Katie understands what he says better than most people.

I always knew what their names were even though most of the rhymes and stories are written in Katie's voice. Three other very important characters, apart from Mum and Dad and Grandma and Grandpa, are here too: Ginger the cat, Buster the dog,

and Bemily, Katie's favourite toy. She is not quite a hippo and not quite a bear, and is based on an old velvet creature who inhabited the bottom of the toy box in our house for many  years. Now she sleeps in her own little bed next to Katie's and they go everywhere together.

This book is all about very real things like mud, sand, water and grass, sunny days and windy ones and the colours of the rainbow. And best of all, playing together. My good friends at Walker Books have given this whole collection a fresh look, and I hope that at least some of the great pleasure I had in writing and illustrating it will rub off on my small readers, and those who read to them.

Shirley Hughes

Chatting

I like chatting.

I chat to the cat,

and I chat
in the car.

I chat with
friends in
the park,

and to the lady at the
supermarket.

Grown-ups like
chatting too.

Sometimes these
chats go on for
rather a long time.

The lady next door is an
especially good chatter.

When Mum is busy she says
that there are just too many
chatterboxes around.

So I go off and
chat to Bemily –
but she never
says a word.

The baby likes
a chat on his toy
telephone. He makes
a lot of calls.

But I can chat to
Grandma and Grandpa
on the real telephone.

Some of the best chats
of all are with Dad, when he
comes to say good night.

Mudlarks

I like mud.
The slippy, sloppy, squelchy kind,

The slap-it-into-pies kind.

Stir it up in puddles,
Slither and slide.

I *do* like mud.

Out and About

Shiny boots,
Brand new,
Pale shoots
Poking through.
In the garden,
Out and about,
Run down the path,
Scamper and shout.
Wild white washing
Waves at the sky,
The birds are busy
And so am I.

I Like Green

Grasshoppers, greenflies, gooseberries, cat's eyes.

Green lettuce, green peas,

Green shade from green trees.
And grass as far as you can see
Like green waves in a green sea.

Playing

Watch me slide,
Slither and glide!

See how
I can throw!

Blowing bubbles –
Look how many!

Running –
Here I go!

Walking my baby,
Just us two.

Watch out for monsters –
They could get you!

I can hop,

 I can skip,

 I can climb
up a chair

Or do balancing tricks
With one foot in the air.

When I hide from the baby
He thinks it's fine,

But when *he* hides from *me*
He's there all the time!

Spring Greens

Bulbs in pots,

Twigs in jars,

Dads in the street, washing cars.

Greens in season,

Trees in bud,

Sky in puddles,

Ripples in mud.

Birds in bushes, singing loud,

Sun tucked up in a bed of cloud.

Water

I like water.
The shallow, splashy, paddly kind,
The hold-on-tight-it's-deep kind.

Slosh it out of buckets,
Spray it all around.

I *do* like water.

Hiding

You can't see me, I'm hiding!

Here I am.

I'm hiding again!
Bet you can't find me this time!

Under a bush in the garden is
a very good place to hide.
So is a big umbrella,

or down at the
end of the bed.

Sometimes Dad hides
behind a newspaper.

And Mum hides
behind a book
on the sofa.

You can even hide
under a hat.

Tortoises hide inside their shells when they aren't feeling friendly.

And hamsters hide right at the back of their cages when they want to go to sleep.

When the baby hides his eyes he thinks you can't see him. But he's there all the time!

A lot of things
seem to hide –
the moon behind
the clouds ...

and the sun
behind the trees.

Flowers need to hide in the
ground in wintertime.

But they come peeping out
again in the spring.

Buster always hides when
it's time for his bath,

and so does Mum's purse when
we're all ready to go out shopping.

Our favourite place to hide is behind the
kitchen door. Then we jump out – BOO!

And can you guess
who's hiding behind
these curtains?

You're right!
Now we're coming out –
is everyone clapping?

Two Shoes, New Shoes

Two shoes, new shoes,
Bright shiny blue shoes.

High-heeled ladies' shoes
For standing tall,

Button-up baby's shoes,
Soft and small.

Slippers,
  warm by the fire,

Lace-ups in the street.

Gloves are for hands
And socks are for feet.

A crown in a cracker,
A hat with a feather,

Sun hats, fun hats,
Hats for bad weather.

A clean white T-shirt
Laid on the bed,

Two holes for arms,
And one for the head.

Zip up a zipper,
Button a coat,

A shoe for a bed,
A hat for a boat.

Wearing it short
And wearing it long,

Getting it right …

And getting it wrong.

Trailing finery,
Dressed for a ball,

And into the bath
Wearing nothing at all!

I Like Blue

Baby blues, navy blues, blue socks, blue shoes,

Blue plate, blue mug, blue flowers in a blue jug.

And fluffy white clouds floating by
In a great big beautiful bright blue sky.

Squirting Rainbows

Bare legs,
Bare toes,
Paddling pool,
Garden hose.
Daisies sprinkled
In the grass,
Dandelions
Bold as brass.
Squirting rainbows,
Sunbeam flashes,
Backyards full
Of shrieks and splashes!

Keeping Busy

Painting a picture,
For everyone to see.

Building a castle –
How high will it be?

Raising a dust cloud,
Sweeping the floor.

Making squelchy sandpies
On the seashore.

Keeping step – left, right –
Marching together.

Stamping in the mud and damp,
Who cares about the weather?

Chatting on the telephone –
Is anybody there?

Bouncing high and showing off
With both feet in the air.

Hammering in the wooden pegs,
Hitting each with care.

Eating up my supper
On my own little chair.

Stretching out with both hands,
Catching the ball.

Then resting on a cushion,
Doing nothing at all.

Sunshine at Bedtime

Streets full of blossom,
Like pink and white snow,
Beds full of tulips,
Tucked up in a row.

Trees full of "candles"
Alight in the park,
Sunshine at bedtime,
Why isn't it dark?

Yet high in the sky
I saw the moon,
Pale as a ghost
In the afternoon.

Hill

Huge clouds
Slowly pass;
Huge hill
Made of grass.
Jungle under,
Thick and green,
Tangled stalks –
Creep between;
Scramble up,
Hug the ground ...

Suddenly see
All around!
Watch out, fences,
Fields and town!
From the top of the world
I come rolling down.

Sand

I like sand.
The run-between-your-fingers kind,
The build-it-into-castles kind.
Mountains of sand meeting the sky,
Flat sand, going on for ever,
I *do* like sand.

I Like Yellow

Syrup dripping
from a spoon,

Buttercups,

A harvest moon.

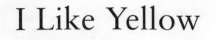

Sun like honey on the floor,
Warm as the steps by our back door.

The Grass House

The grass house
Is my private place.
Nobody can see me
In the grass house.
Feathery plumes
Meet over my head.
Down here,
In the green, there are:
Seeds
Weeds
Stalks
Pods
And tiny little flowers.

Only the cat
And some busy, hurrying ants
Know where my grass house is.

Seaside

Sand in the sandwiches,
Sand in the tea,
Flat, wet sand running
Down to the sea.
Pools full of seaweed,
Shells and stones,
Damp bathing suits
And ice-cream cones.

Waves pouring in
To a sandcastle moat.
Mend the defences!
Now we're afloat!
Water's for splashing,
Sand is for play,
A day by the sea
Is the best kind of day.

Giving

I gave Mum a present on her birthday,
all wrapped up in pretty paper.
And she gave me a big kiss.

I gave Dad a very special picture which I painted at playgroup. And he gave me a ride on his shoulders most of the way home.

I gave the baby some slices
of my apple.

We ate them sitting under the table.

At teatime the baby gave me
two of his soggy crusts.

That wasn't much of a present!

You can give someone
a cross look ...

or a big smile!

74

You can give a tea party ...

or a seat on a crowded bus.

On my birthday Grandma and Grandpa
gave me a beautiful doll's pram.
I said "Thank you" and gave
them each a big hug.

And I gave my dear Bemily
a ride in it, all the way
down the garden path
and back again.

I tried to give the cat a
ride too, but she gave me
a nasty scratch!

So Dad had to give
my poor arm a kiss and
a wash and a piece
of sticking plaster.

Sometimes, just when
I've built a big castle
out of bricks,

the baby comes along and
gives it a big swipe!
And it all falls down.

Then I feel like giving
the baby a big
swipe too.

But I don't, because he *is*
my baby brother, after all.

Helping

Cooking the dinner,
Stirring the pot.

Time for a taste
If it isn't too hot!

Pouring out water.
Oops! What a mess!

Washing hands all by myself –
Can I reach? Yes!

Counting for the baby,

Stroking the cat,

Tearing up this,

And tidying that.

Standing up straight –
Can you do it on your own?

Keep still – I'm measuring!
My, how you've grown!

Teaching the class –
Pay attention everyone!

And now it's time for tickling.
Let's have fun!

Wind

I like the wind.
The soft, summery, gentle kind,
The gusty, blustery, fierce kind.
Ballooning out the curtains,
Blowing things about,
Wild and wilful everywhere.
I *do* like the wind.

When We Went to the Park

When Grandpa
and I put on our coats
and went to the park ...

We saw one black cat
sitting on a wall,

Two big girls
licking ice-creams,

Three ladies chatting
on a bench,

Four babies
in buggies,

Five children
playing in the
sandpit,

Six runners running,

Seven dogs chasing one another,

Eight boys
kicking a ball,

Nine ducks swimming
on the pond,

Ten birds swooping
in the sky,

And so many leaves
that I couldn't count
them all.

On the way back we
saw the black cat again.
Then we went home
for tea.

I Like Orange

Tangerines and apricots,
Orange flowers in orange pots.

Orange glow on an orange mat,
Marmalade toast and a marmalade cat.

93

Misty

Mist in the morning,
Raw and nippy,
Leaves on the pavement,
Wet and slippy.
Sun on fire
Behind the trees,
Muddy boots,
Muddy knees.

Shop windows,
Lighted early,
Soaking grass,
Dewy, pearly.
Red, lemon,
Orange and brown,
Silently, softly,
The leaves float down.

Being Together

Telling a secret,
Listening with care,

Bending down low,
Stretching high in the air.

Dancing to music,
Feeling the beat,

Lying flat on our backs
And kicking our feet.

Laughing
(Always a good thing to do),

Reading out loud,
Reading to you.

Sharing a sandwich,

A new place to hide.

Love and kisses
And two smiles wide!

Feasts

Apples heaped on market barrows,
Juicy plums and stripy marrows.

Grains of barley,
Carefully stored,

Feasts of berries,

Nuts to hoard,

And ripe pumpkins, yellow and green,
To light with candles at Hallowe'en.

I Like Black

Shiny boots,
A witch's hat.
Black cloak,
Black cat.

Black crows cawing high,
Winter trees against the sky.

Bouncing

When I throw my big shiny ball ...

it bounces away from me.

Bounce, bounce, bounce, bounce!

Then it rolls along the ground, then it stops.

I like bouncing too.

In the mornings I bounce on my bed,
and the baby bounces in his cot.

Mum and Dad's big bed is an
even better place to bounce.

But Dad doesn't much like being
bounced on in the early morning.

So we roll on the floor instead, and
the baby bounces on ME!

After breakfast he
does some dancing
in his baby-bouncer,

and I do some dancing
to the radio.

At my playgroup there are big cushions
on the floor where lots of children
can bounce together.

And at home there's
a big sofa where we
can bounce when
Mum isn't looking.

Grandpa and I know a good bouncing game.
I ride on his knees and we sing:

*This is the way
the ladies ride:
trit-trot, trit-trot;*

*This is the way
the gentlemen ride:
tarran, tarran;*

*This is the way
the farmers ride:
clip-clop, clip-clop;*

*This is the way
the jockeys ride:
gallopy, gallopy ... and FALL OFF!*

I like bouncing.

I bounce about all day ...

bounce,
    bounce,
    bounce,
    bounce!

Until in the end I stop bouncing,
and go off to sleep.

Fire

Fire is a dragon
(Better beware),
Dangerous and beautiful
(Better take care).
Puffing out smoke
As soon as it's lit,
Licking up leaves,
Crackle and spit!

Sending up sparks
Into the sky
That hover a moment
And suddenly die.
Fire is a dragon,
Alive in the night;
Fiery dragon,
Glittering bright.

I Like Red

Rosy apples, dark cherries,

Scarlet leaves, bright berries.

And when the winter's day is done,
A fiery sky, a big red sun.

Hoping

Grey day,
Dark at four,
Hurry home,
Shut the door.
Think of a time
When there will be
Decorations
On a tree,
Tangerines,
And hot mince pies,
A bulging stocking,
A Christmas surprise!

Cold

Cold fingers,
Cold toes,
Pink sky,
Pink nose.
Hard ground,
Bare trees,
Branches crack,
Puddles freeze.
Frost white,
Sun red,
Warm room,
Warm bed.

I Like White

Thistledown like white fluff,
Dandelion clocks to puff.
White cover on my bed,
White pillow for my head.

White snowflakes, whirling down,
Covering gardens, roofs and town.

Noisy

Noisy noises!
Pan lids clashing,

Dog barking,
Plate smashing,

Telephone ringing,
Baby bawling,

Midnight cats
Cat-a-wauling,

Door slamming,
Aeroplane zooming,

Vacuum cleaner
Vroom-vroom-vrooming,

And if I dance and sing a tune,
Baby joins in with a saucepan
and spoon.

Gentle noises ...
Dry leaves swishing,

Falling rain,
Splashing, splishing,

Rustling trees,
Hardly stirring,

Lazy cat
Softly purring.

Story's over,
Bedtime's come,

Crooning baby
Sucks his thumb.

All quiet, not a peep,

Everyone is fast asleep.